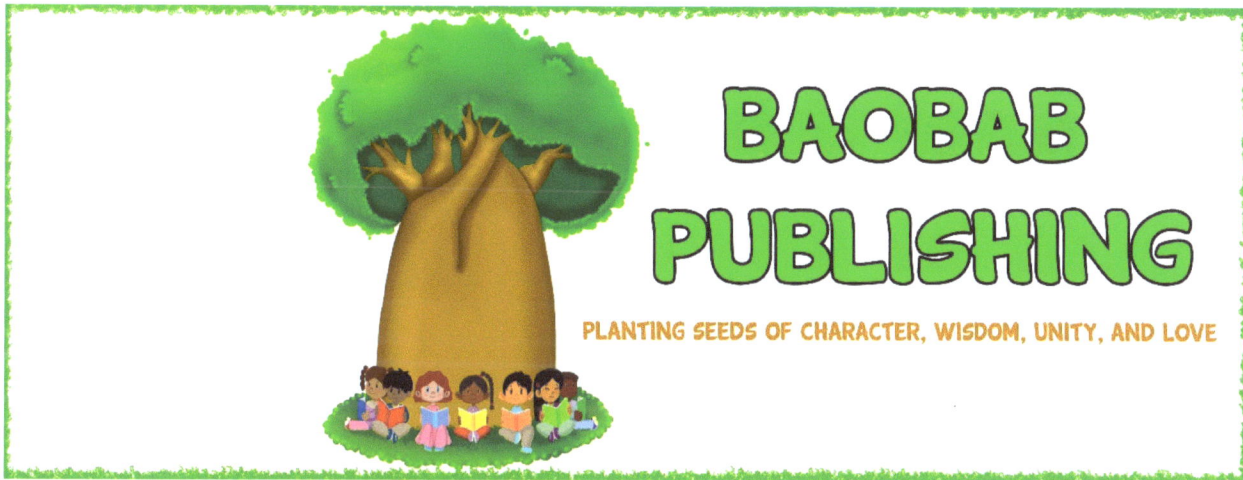

BAOBAB PUBLISHING

PLANTING SEEDS OF CHARACTER, WISDOM, UNITY, AND LOVE

Text and Illustrations Copyright © 2015 by Schertevear Q. Watkins and Susieann Beavers Harris.

Address all inquiries to:

Baobab Books

Email: bbfbooks@gmail.com

ISBN-13:
978-0692689578 (Baobab Publishing)

ISBN-10:
0692689575

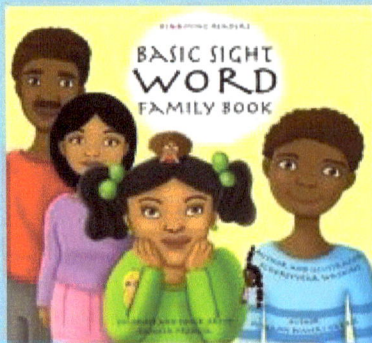

BEGINNING READERS

BASIC SIGHT
WORD
FAMILY BOOK

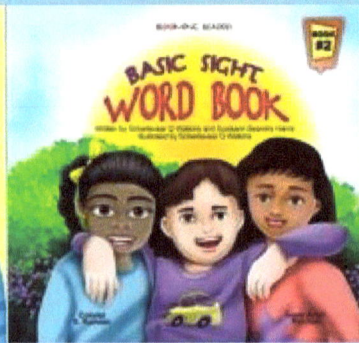

BOOK-IN-C READER
Book #2

BASIC SIGHT
WORD BOOK

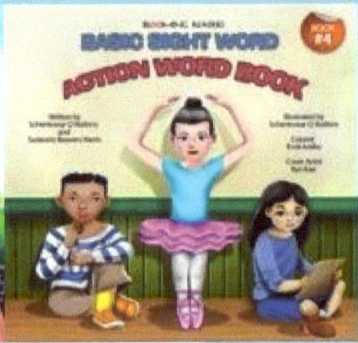

BOOK-IN-C READER
Book #4

BASIC SIGHT WORD
ACTION WORD BOOK

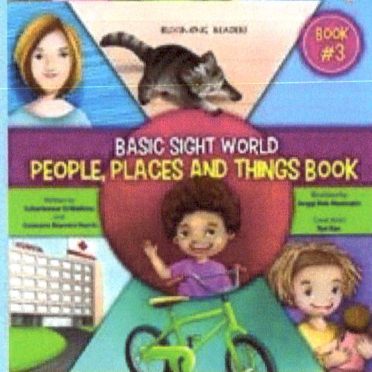

BEGINNING READERS
Book #3

BASIC SIGHT WORLD
PEOPLE, PLACES AND THINGS BOOK

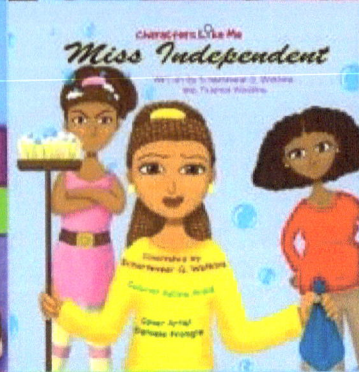

Characters Like Me

Miss Independent

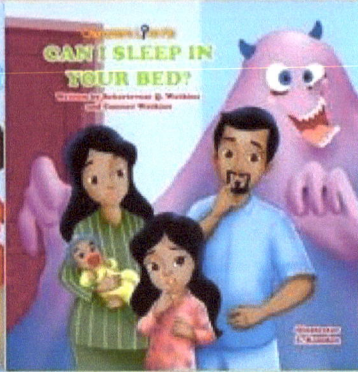

Characters Like Me

CAN I SLEEP IN
YOUR BED?

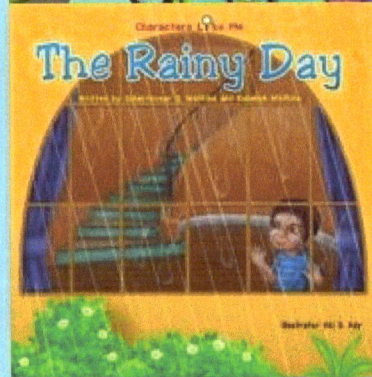

Characters Like Me

The Rainy Day

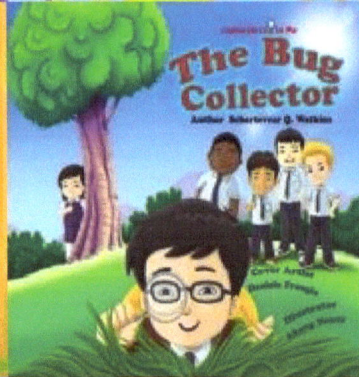

Characters Like Me

The Bug
Collector

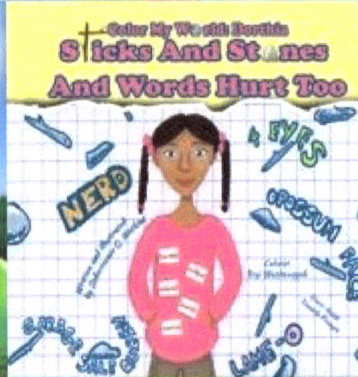

Color My Words with Emotion

Sticks And Stones
And Words Hurt Too

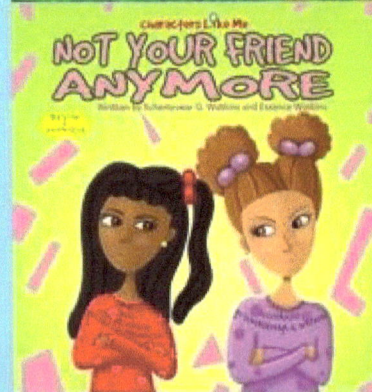

Characters Like Me

NOT YOUR FRIEND
ANYMORE

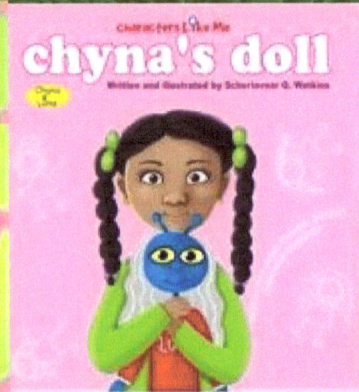

Characters Like Me

chyna's doll

Written and Illustrated by Schartevear G. Watkins

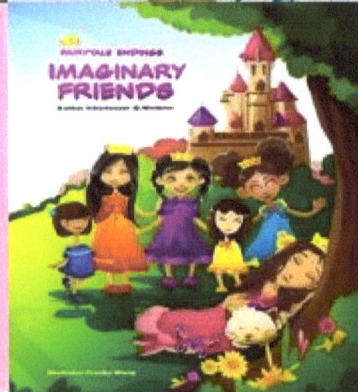

Fairytale Express

IMAGINARY
FRIENDS

About The Authors

SCHERTEVEAR WATKINS

With a career in Early Child Hood Education and as a divorced single mother, Schertevear Watkins' love for children has inspired her to dedicating her life to bringing positive influences into the lives of as many children as possible.

In the summer of 2014 Schertevear Watkins launched The Village Online Community website in an effort to make it easier for parents to find Private Schools, Arts Programs, Special Needs Services, and Recreation for all children across Georgia. This year she is continuing to reach out to children and families through positive literature which will include books that promote learning, character development, social skills, family and more.

SUSIEANN BEAVERS HARRIS

As a former Pre-kindergarten transition coach Susieann Beavers-Harris is an advocate for early childhood education. She also worked as a volunteer in Pre-K classrooms where she saw first-hand the areas most challenging to early learners.

Knowing that there are so many children that need the extra practice to prepare them for elementary school has inspired Ms. Beavers-Harris to do as much as she can to help prepare today's children for a successful tomorrow.

Action Words tell what something or someone is doing. Action words are called **verbs.** In this book you will learn to recognize many action words as you read about what many people and things are doing.

running   sliding   jumping

Rita likes to **swing** high.

Zac can **slide** down fast.

Wanda loves to **swim** in the pool.

See Spot **run** through the grass.

Pete and Vicky **color** the pictures.

Opal loves to **talk** on the phone.

Chad likes to **drink** milk with cookies.

Ben **hides** and Lee will **seek.**

Look at Joe **eat** his lunch.

Erin **plays** with her dolls.

Pam loves to **read** books.

See Eddie **sit** and **build** in the sand.

They **ride** on the school bus.

Watch Fanny **dance** at her ballet recital.

Grandma has to **use** a walker.

Daddy and Lisa **skate** in the park.

Xena can **jump** real high.

Listen to Gary **sing** and play his guitar.

Tim likes to **paint** his hands.

Kim can **write** numbers.

Mom and Sid **walk** in the park.

Bo can **count** to three.

Action Word List

Swing	Slide	Swim
Run	Color	Talk
Drink	Hides	Seek
Eat	Plays	Read
Sit	Build	Ride
Dance	Use	Skate
Jump	Sing	Paint
Write	Count	Look
See	Watch	Listen

More To Learn

Using The Book

- How to use this book- Read this book with your early reader. Touch the words in bold as you read them. Ask your child to show you the character in the book that displays the action in bold.
- Make it fun and relatable - Ask questions as you read to your child. "Do you like to swing like Rita?" or "What is Joe eating for lunch?" or "Who do you like to talk to on the phone?" or "Have you ever jumped as high as Xena?"
- Reading Ready - When your child is ready, allow him / her to read to you. Starting out you may want to alternate the pages. You may read all the pages on the left and he/ she read the pages on the right.

Beyond The Book

- To give your child more practice with the sight words introduced in this book, try making flash cards.
- What you'll need-All you need is a black marker and blank index cards or sentence strips.
- What to do-Write a sight word on each card. No picture needed.
- How to use- If your goal is to teach your child the words in this book, read the book at least twice a week with your child. Also, review the sight word flash cards with your child at least three times a week for about five minutes.
- Something to Consider-No need for a picture. Letters are, in a sense pictures. Often times when children use illustrated flash cards they are looking at the picture and not the word. The picture becomes a distraction for some children.

The Series

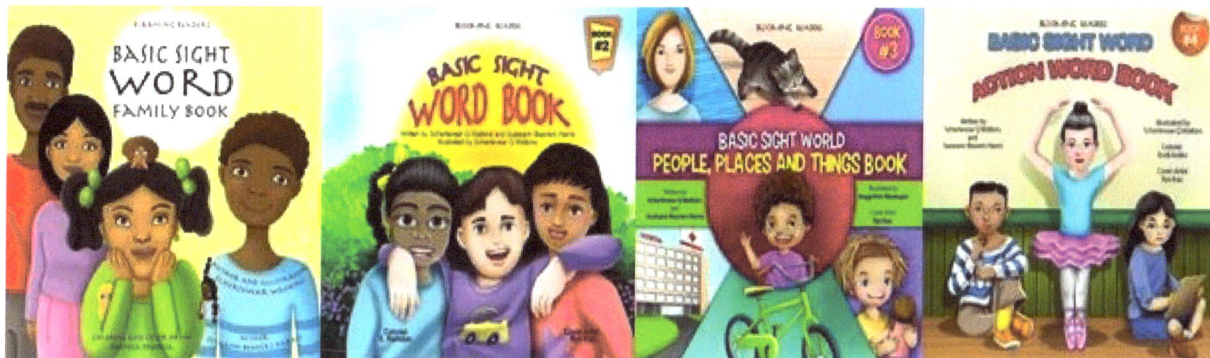

Blooming readers is not just a random series of books. It is a unique Early Reading Tool. When books are purchased in order, the sight words given in our books can all be put together to form hundreds of sentences. Try playing sentence games by putting noun, verb and adjective words together using your flashcards to make sentences your child can read because they will already know the words from previous Blooming Readers books.

Try the additional activities on the following pages for extra practice.

Activity
Circle The **Action Word** of **Verb** In Each Row

1)   cat   look   pretty

2)   sing   toy   book

3)   rock   heavy   play

4)   frog   cry   hard

5)   girl   twist   clock

6)   desk   flip   mean

Circle The **Action Words** or **Verbs** in Each Sentence

Parents may help kids read the sentences if needed.

1) She fell off of the bed.
2) The boy ran really fast.
3) My dad works late sometimes.
4) Mom cooks breakfast every morning.
5) I like to skip across the grass.
6) My sister plays school.
7) Fred ate all of his cabbage.
8) The toad leaped up high.
9) I watch television sometimes
10) Carry flies her kite in the wind.

www.ingramcontent.com/pod-product-compliance
Lightning Source LLC
Chambersburg PA
CBHW042106040426
42448CB00002B/167